W9-ATR-558

Language Teaching Techniques

Resource Handbook Number 1
Second, Revised Edition

Raymond C. Clark

Illustrations by Patrick R. Moran

PRO LINGUA  ASSOCIATES

Publishers

Other handbooks in this series:
The ESL Miscellany
Experiential Language Teaching Techniques
Cultural Awareness Teaching Techniques
Technology Assisted Teaching Techniques

Published by Pro Lingua Associates
15 Elm Street
Brattleboro, Vermont 05301

SAN 216-0579

802-257-7779

Second, revised edition

Copyright © 1980, 1987 by Raymond C. Clark

ISBN 0-86647-023-9

Library of Congress Cataloguing in Publication Data:

Clark, Raymond C.   1937-
Language teaching techniques.

(Resource handbook - Pro Lingua Associates ; no. 1)
1. Language, Modern—Study and teaching
2. Communicative competence—Study and teaching.
I. Title. II. Series: Pro Lingua Associates.
Resource handbook - Pro Lingua Associates ; no. 1.
PB35.C547   418'.007   80-84109

Printed in the United States of America

3rd Printing 1987
9,000 copies in print

Acknowledgements

A book such as this one probably contains little that is truly original. However, in the Notes section of the techniques I have tried to give credit where I believe it is due. I hope I have not committed any glaring errors of omission. In case I have, I would defend myself by saying that in the twelve years that I was on the staff of the School for International Training, I met, talked with, listened to, observed and worked with hundreds of language teachers, students and scholars, and it is not always possible to sort out the exact particulars of where I first learned about a specific teaching technique or procedure. In many cases, I have probably modified somebody else's idea to fit my own style. In some cases I may have invented a label to describe a technique that other people may know under a different name.

If I may claim any originality, I believe that "Characters in Search of an Author," "Grid Drill," and "Spontaneous Pattern Practice" are techniques that I "invented." The point of this book, however, is not to sort out the inventors of these various techniques, if there are any, but rather to bring them together in a format that is clear, simple and useful.

In the first paragraph I mentioned the many language teachers, students and scholars who have passed through the School for International Training. I am indebted to all of them for contributing directly and indirectly to my own repertoire of techniques which have formed the basis for this book. I cannot possibly list them, but I do thank them and I especially thank the students of the Master of Arts in Teaching Program.

Secondly, I would like to thank the US Peace Corps and The Experiment in International Living for affording me the opportunity to work as project director and editor for the Peace Corps Language Handbook Series. This assignment enabled me to put into print for the first time the various techniques that I had collected through the years. This present volume is a refinement of the <u>Teacher's Handbook</u> that I wrote for the Peace Corps series.

The following staff members on the Peace Corps project contributed to the development of the original Teacher's Handbook: Andy Burrows, Peg Clement, Jon Dayley, Steve Hanchey, Annie Hawkinson, Dave Hopkins, Thom Huebner, Susan McBean, Pat Moran, Annie Suquet and Steve Trussel. Thanks to all of them.

Special thanks are due to Andy Burrows who wrote first drafts of five of the grammar techniques and who prodded me along the path toward the final development of this book. I also owe Andy thanks for his patient supervision of the final design, composition and production of this book. He also contributed the illustration on page 97.

Thanks also to Susan McBean who typed the final manuscript copy, contributed several suggestions and raised a few questions where they were needed. And thanks to Lisa Forrett for her efficient typesetting.

Finally, I would like to acknowledge the illustrations and companionship of Pat Moran. We had fun and I look forward to our next project together.

Raymond C. Clark

Table of Contents

Language
Teaching
Techniques

Introduction

The techniques in this book should be viewed first and foremost as techniques for improving the student's command of the spoken language. Therefore, listening comprehension and fluent and accurate speaking skills are the principal objectives of these techniques. However, it should be pointed out that many, if not all, of these techniques could and probably should be accompanied by activities that also require the students to use the written language. In many cases in fact, appropriate reading and writing activities are suggested within the description of the technique. There are of course, many language teaching techniques that are designed primarily for improving the student's reading and writing skills, but they are not the subject of this book.

The techniques are divided into two major types: techniques for improving the student's communicative competence (Communication Techniques) and techniques for improving the student's grammatical accuracy (Grammar Techniques). Although the term communicative competence implies that a person who can communicate competently will do so with considerable grammatical accuracy, we are using communicative competence (in contrast to linguistic competence) to include all those communication skills that go beyond merely speaking with grammatical accuracy. These skills include an extensive and appropriate vocabulary, gestures and body language, cross-cultural awareness and sociolinguistically appropriate usage.

This two-part division is based on an approach to language teaching and learning called Interplay. In its simplest form Interplay refers to the practice of encouraging constant interaction among the participants in the eternal triangle of language learning: teacher, student(s), and the language (materials). The Interplay approach also assumes that as a student grapples with the language, he has two main objectives: communicative competence and

1

grammatical accuracy, and although these two objectives are ultimately inseparable and equally important, at any given moment in the language learning process, the student can focus on only one of these objectives. The language program (and its materials) should take this into account by being organized in such a way as to allow constant interplay between grammatical and communicative work.

In practice, of course, grammar techniques frequently incorporate activities that are somewhat communicative in nature, and communication techniques will often involve rather systematic and repetitive practice with specific grammatical items. However, we believe it would be useful for the teacher to keep this grammar-communication dichotomy distinct in his own mind. There may be times, for example, when the students want or need to focus their attention on a specific grammatical pattern. At these times, systematic <u>practice</u> (Grammar Techniques) is required. Conversely, when the students need or want practice in using the language in a realistic way, the rigid structure of grammar drills would be inappropriate and activities that require the student to <u>use</u> the language (Communication Techniques) should be employed. Needless to say, any learner of a language must develop both grammatical accuracy and communicative skill, and so an integrated language program will demand work in both areas. In yet another application of the Interplay approach, it should be up to the teacher and the students working together to decide how and when to mix these two types of work to insure that the language program is comprehensive and relevant to the needs of the students.

Within both major types of activities there is also a general progression from tightly controlled activities which are frequently teacher-centered to less-controlled activities which allow the students to be creative in their explorations of the language. For example, among the grammar techniques, the first one in the list is Substitution Drill where there is only one correct response for the student to make, whereas Manipulations, the last technique in the Grammar list allows the students to respond in a variety of ways. By the same token, among the communication techniques, the first one in the list (Ritual) is a pre-established language sample which the students are usually expected to memorize while the Constructalog technique, in many ways similar to a ritual, encourages the students to write their own language samples.

The format in which the various techniques are presented is rather self-explanatory. The basic information

(Purpose, Brief Description and Sample Text) is presented on the first page. The middle pages contain an illustration and the basic procedure. Inexperienced teachers will probably spend most of their time reading and thinking about this essential information. The next two sections, (Variations and Suggestions and Guidelines for Developing Your Own Material) will be of interest to the experienced teacher who may already be familiar with the basic procedures. We have also endeavored to present the techniques as clearly and simply as possible so that they will be accessible to both the native speaker of English and to the many language teachers, both in the US and abroad, who may not speak English as their first language.

Finally, it should be pointed out that this collection of techniques is eclectic in nature. It is not intended to present any particular method of language teaching. If the techniques have anything in common, it is that they have proven to be successful and useful. Furthermore, this collection of techniques should not be viewed as a methods textbook; it is a resource book that <u>describes</u> several teaching techniques. It does not <u>prescribe</u> how to teach a second/foreign language; that is another subject for another day. And this collection is in no way comprehensive; it is a limited selection of basic techniques for teaching the spoken language.

It might be helpful to view this collection of techniques as a collection of basic tools, somewhat analogous to a carpenter's tool box. Each tool is useful for specific purposes, but just as a house cannot be built with a hammer alone, neither can a good language program be fashioned from an over-reliance on any one technique or an indiscriminate use of these teaching techniques.

Pro Lingua Associates

Ritual

To have the students memorize set phrases, sentences, or sequences of sentences because (1) the lines are highly predictable and therefore useful in general conversation or (2) because the lines contain idiomatic expressions or other "frozen" pieces of language such as greetings or (3) because the lines contain useful examples of a particular grammatical construction and can therefore serve as model sentences for future reference.

BRIEF DESCRIPTION:

A ritual is a brief conversation. Usually it centers around a common everyday activity involving two people. Because it is intended to be a memorization activity, typically the ritual is composed of short sentences in a very limited number of exchanges. The longer the ritual is, the more unwieldy it becomes for memorization purposes.

SAMPLE RITUAL:

A: Excuse me teacher, do you mind if I smoke?
B: I'm sorry, there's no smoking in the classroom.

A: Oh, I didn't know.
B: Don't worry about it.

PROCEDURE:

1. Present the ritual while the students listen. Repeat it two or three times using gestures, pictures, puppets, etc. to help convey the identity of the speaker and the meaning of the ritual.

2. Ask the students questions about the ritual. This is to make sure that they understand the general sense of the ritual as well as the meaning of individual words.

3. Have the students read the ritual and allow them to ask questions.

4. You say a line and the students repeat the same line. Do this several times for each line until you have practiced repeating the entire ritual.

5. You take part A and the students take part B. You say the first line and the students respond with the second line. This is done for each pair of lines until the students can respond easily.

6. Reverse the parts. The students initiate the ritual with Part A and you respond.

7. Have the students practice the ritual in pairs. Move around the room listening and correcting.

8. Have pairs of students perform the ritual to the rest of the class.

VARIATIONS:

1. Instead of having the students read the ritual in the book, write it on the board. As you repeat and practice the ritual, erase it word by word until nothing remains.

2. In Step 4 (repetitions), vary the repetitions from individual responses to choral responses.

3. Instead of having the students see the written version of the ritual in Step 3 (read), have them try to write it out before they have seen the written version. One student can go to the board and write the sentences while the other students contribute the lines, spelling them as best as they can. You would correct the students' spelling as you go along.

4. When you have finished all 7 steps, give the ritual as a dictation. You read a line and the students write it down. Check their work. Re-creating a written version of the ritual can be a useful "test" of whether the students have learned the ritual well.

5. Have the students re-tell the ritual as a narrative. For example, the re-telling might begin: "The student asked the teacher if he could smoke." etc.

6. Use stick figures to cue the students on the sequence of the ritual. The following sequence represents the sample ritual. Note the key:

   + = an affirmative statement   ? = a question

   - = a negative statement   ! = an imperative.

SUGGESTIONS AND GUIDELINES for Writing a Ritual:

1. Keep the lines short: no more than 8-10 words per line.

2. Keep the ritual short: 4-10 lines.

3. Avoid a three-person ritual wherever possible.

4. Try to write the ritual in sub-sections. Pairs of statements or questions with accompanying response is an easy pattern to work with.

5. Keep the conversation natural and colloquial. Do your lines reflect what people actually say in the given situation?

6. The following topics/situations can be cast in a ritualistic format:

   * greetings and leave-takings
     -- "Hello, how are you?..."

   * street directions
     -- "Excuse me, where is ..."

   * introductions of people
     -- "John, I'd like you to meet ..."

   * simple inquiries for information
     -- "Excuse me, can you tell me ..."

   * buying/bargaining for something
     -- "How much is that ..."

   * brief conversational rituals
     -- "Nice day, isn't it? ..."

   * classroom rituals
     -- "Teacher, how do you spell ..."

NOTES:

1. A ritual is a variation of the well-known and over-used language teaching practice of using dialogues for memorization. This Ritual technique is based on Alexander Lipson's use of rituals in A Russian Course. Cambridge, Mass: Slavica Publishers Inc., 1974.

2. Classroom rituals like the sample can be used over and over whenever they are appropriate. Lipson often introduces humor into his rituals and encourages students to initiate rituals whenever the opportunity is available.

A Special Note ———————————————————————

On Rituals, Dialogues and Mini-Dramas

You may have wondered about the difference between a ritual, a dialogue and a mini-drama (page 31). You may also have noticed that there is no technique labelled Dialogue in this collection, even though language textbooks abound with dialogues.

To be sure, rituals, dialogues and mini-dramas are similar and for that matter they could all be labelled conversations. In this book, however, they are considered to be distinct from each other; the following definitions may help clarify that distinction.

Rituals are very short conversations that are frequently repeated in everyday situations. They are repetitive in nature and rarely convey much real information. Students are expected to memorize rituals because they are useful.

Mini-Dramas. Are long conversations (or very short dramas or playlets) that frequently tell a story. They represent the spoken language in written form, and therefore, they are of interest to the language student because they are samples of authentic language use. However, because they are long and unique (the opposite of repetitive) they are not to be memorized.

Dialogues are typically halfway between rituals and mini-dramas. They are short, but usually longer than a ritual. They often contain ritualistic elements, but they also usually convey some unique information or tell a very simple story. Dialogues can be useful samples of authentic language and therefore dialogues can be the basis for an interesting class. However, the traditional way of teaching a dialogue has centered around memorizing the dialogue--a practice that is of very limited usefulness.

We have chosen not to present dialogues as a separate technique in this book because we feel that the purposes of the language learner can be better served through the use of rituals and/or mini-dramas.

Cummings Device

To have the students practice useful, high-frequency sentences and variations of those sentences. Typically, these sentences are in question-answer pairs and will allow the student to ask for and receive simple information.

BRIEF DESCRIPTION:

This technique is similar to a ritual or dialogue, but it is usually shorter (4-6 lines) and it has "holes" in the dialogue where words and/or phrases are to be put in. The words and phrases are listed separately from the sentences.

SAMPLE CUMMINGS DEVICE:

A: What time does the bus leave?
B: It leaves at _____I_____ .

A: Which gate does it leave from?
B: It leaves from gate _____II_____ .

I

one o'clock,
quarter past one,
half past one,
quarter to one,
five minutes to one, etc.

II

Twenty-one
Twenty-two
Twenty-three
etc.

PROCEDURE:

1. Present the conversation to be sure the students understand the meaning.

2. Go through the list of words and phrases to make sure the students understand them.

3. Have the students repeat the lines after you, as in a simple repetition practice.

4. Have the students respond. You take one part and the student responds with the other. Then change parts.

5. Have the students practice the conversation with each other while you listen and make corrections.

VARIATIONS:

1. The practice can be done with or without open books. It is usually best to do it first with open books and then have the students do it with books closed.

2. You can put the list of words and phrases on the board.

3. Frequently these exercises can be done with actual objects, or actual information such as a bus schedule.

4. If the practice goes easily and quickly, add more vocabulary items or extend the Cummings Device to another pair of utterances.

5. Have the students put the Cummings Device in the context of a longer conversation, using greetings and other phrases they may have learned, such as "excuse me," "thank you," etc.

SUGGESTIONS AND GUIDELINES for Cummings Devices:

1. Two question-answer pairs of 8-10 words per line is a good device.

2. Approximately one dozen pieces of information is sufficient (6 items per blank).

3. Good conversation starters for a Cummings Device are question words (who, when, where, how long, how far).

4. Many good Cummings Devices can be developed for use with schedules, charts, maps, and other lists of information. The information source can be reproduced on the board or as handouts. Some suggested sources of information are:

   * bus, plane, and train schedules

   * tariff and fare tables

   * postage rate charts from a post office

   * maps, especially highway mileage maps

   * weather reports from the newspaper

   * sports score reports

   * movie advertisements from the movie page in a newspaper

   * other newspaper information summaries such as ship movements in and out of a port, temperatures from selected cities around the world, astrology columns

   * statistics, charts, and tables from books such as The World Almanac.

NOTE:

The term Cummings Device was first used by Earl W. Stevick to describe a lesson format derived from the practices of Thomas Cummings, as described in Cummings' book How to Learn a Foreign Language. For a more complete description see Earl W. Stevick, Adapting and Writing Language Lessons. Foreign Service Institute (Superintendent of Documents; U.S. Government Printing Office, Washington, D.C.: 1971), pp. 310-315.

Recitation

PURPOSE:

    To provide the students with a string of sentences which will be the basis for a conversation that can be used to explain, describe or justify oneself to a native speaker.

BRIEF DESCRIPTION:

    The students memorize a short series of sentences. The sentences are not intended to be recited verbatim in a real conversation. Individual sentences within the recitation can be used, however, in real conversation. Frequently the recitation is personalized.

SAMPLE RECITATION:

My name is _____ .

I'm from _____ .

I'm a _____ .

I'm _____ years old.

I was born _____ .

15

PROCEDURE:

1. Present the recitation using information about yourself.

2. Make sure the students understand the meaning of each sentence.

3. Go through the recitation sentence by sentence. Give each student the information he/she needs. In many cases, the students will be able to supply their own information.

4. Have each student write out his/her recitation.

5. Have each student memorize the recitation. They should start off by studying their recitations individually.

6. The students can practice their recitations in pairs while you circulate, listening for errors.

7. Each student can present his/her recitation to the rest of the class.

VARIATIONS:

1. You can make up a question that goes with each line in the recitation and have the students learn to respond correctly to each question. Vary the order of the questions.

2. The students can also learn the questions and ask each other.

3. The students can try to do recitations based on the other people in the class. This would force them to practice 3rd person (he/she) forms.

4. Have the students add more sentences to the recitation.

SUGGESTIONS AND GUIDELINES for Writing a Recitation:

1. Concentrate on personal information or on information which is of high interest to the learner, such as a description of his/her job.

2. If the recitation is to be memorized, 6-8 lines should be sufficient.

3. A useful topic of conversation for language learners is one that begins with the phrase "In my country, we _____...." Recitations can be used to provide people with things to say. Conversations of this type are a first step toward cross-cultural communication.

4. Some other topics that could be developed into recitations are:

   * My family
   * My hometown
   * My job/assignment
   * My impressions of your country
   * Daily/weekly/seasonal routines
   * The climate in my country
   * Various cultural events such as holidays, celebrations, weddings, funerals, etc.
   * Personal interests and hobbies.

Narrative

To use a narrative passage as a basis for practicing the language by talking about the passage. The students may also learn new vocabulary and to a lesser extent, grammatical features.

BRIEF DESCRIPTION:

A narrative is a short descriptive paragraph. It can be an informational text on some aspect of the culture taken from primary sources such as newspapers, magazines and books or it can be purposefully written to introduce new vocabulary or grammatical features.

A narrative is not intended to be conversational and it is not to be memorized. Because it contains several sentences strung together in a paragraph it is a useful device for introducing the student to words and phrases that are extra-sentential, such as 'however,' 'although,' 'this' and 'it' (referring to something in a previous sentence).

SAMPLE NARRATIVE:

Winter in Vermont usually lasts five months. It begins when the first snow falls. Frequently the first snow-fall comes early in December, but occasionally the first snow comes before Thanksgiving. The snow remains on the ground until April. Winter is important to the economy of Vermont because thousands of people come to Vermont to ski.

PROCEDURE:

Before teaching a narrative, go over it and circle the words you want to ask questions about. Here are four kinds of questions you can ask:

a. Question-word questions (How long does it last?) Other question words are what, who, which, when, where, how and why.

b. Yes-No questions (Does it last five months?).

c. Either-Or questions (Does it last four or five months?).

d. Clarification questions using emphasis or statements with question intonation (FIVE months?) or (It lasts FIVE months?).

1. <u>Read</u> the narrative through once without stopping.

2. <u>Ask</u> general comprehension questions such as "What is <u>this</u> narrative about?"

3. <u>Read</u> <u>the</u> <u>narrative</u> <u>sentence</u> <u>by</u> <u>sentence</u>, stopping at <u>the end</u> of each sentence to <u>ask</u> <u>and</u> <u>answer</u> questions about the sentence (See the Question-Word Analysis technique).

Teacher says:	Student says:
a. Winter in Vermont usually lasts five months.	a. (listens).
b. Which season?	b. Winter
c. Where?	c. In Vermont.
d. How long does it last?	d. Five months.
e. Five <u>years</u>?	e. No, five <u>months</u>.
f. <u>Four</u> months?	f. No, <u>five</u> months.
g. <u>Does</u> it <u>always</u> last five months?	g. No, <u>usually</u> it lasts five months
h. Give me the whole sentence.	h. Winter in Vermon usually lasts five months.

4. <u>Put</u> <u>new</u> <u>words</u> <u>and</u> <u>phrases</u> <u>on</u> <u>the</u> <u>blackboard</u>.

5. <u>Have</u> <u>the</u> <u>students</u> <u>re-create</u> <u>the</u> <u>narrative</u> using the <u>key</u> <u>words</u> from Step 4 as cues. Let each student contribute a sentence. Although nobody will know the entire paragraph verbatim, together the students may be able to reconstruct most of the paragraph.

VARIATIONS:

1. After you read each sentence, have one student ask the questions of the other students.

2. You can have the students follow along in the book at first, and then have them close their books and continue the exercise without seeing the written word.

3. Put the narrative on the board and gradually erase it word by word.

4. At the conclusion of the practice, ask for a volunteer to try to re-tell the entire paragraph. Don't insist on exact memorization. An accurate paraphrase is quite acceptable.

5. Sometimes you can have the students do a parallel narrative. In other words, if the narrative is about some aspect of your culture, you can have the students construct a similar narrative about the same topic in their culture.

SUGGESTIONS AND GUIDELINES for Writing a Narrative:

1. Keep the narrative short: 6-12 lines should be a sufficient challenge.

2. Keep the sentences simple, although with advanced students, the length and complexity of the sentences can be increased.

3. Try to include an average of one new word per sentence. Don't overload the narrative with new vocabulary.

4. Sometimes an interesting picture can be the basis for a narrative.

5. Good primary sources for narratives are:

   * Newspapers. Look for news summaries. You may need to edit the material. Sentences in the newspapers tend to be long and involved.

   * Books. Works of non-fiction are probably more useful. Travelogues with observations on the people and culture could be especially valuable.

   * Magazines. Editing may be necessary.

   * Advertisements.

   * Pamphlets and brochures.

   * Historic markers with short explanatory texts.

6. You can "seed" your own written narratives with certain grammatical features such as:

   * Frequency words (always, never, sometimes,etc.)

   * Connectives (however, although, moreover, nevertheless, etc.)

   * Passive constructions

   * Existential constructions (there is/are)

A Special Note ──────────────────────────────────

On Recitations, Narratives and Prose Passages

The three techniques called Recitations, Narratives, and Prose Passages may at first glance seem to be very similar. Superficially, they are similar in that the basic language sample is in the form of one or more prose paragraphs. However, the nature of the language, the way the class uses the material, and the purposes of the material are somewhat different. The differences are summarized below.

Recitations are short passages that the learner memorizes. The passage is memorized because it is expected that the learner will have occasion to use the entire passage or significant portions of it frequently. The eventual use for a recitation is somewhat analogous to a child learning to recite the national pledge or a daily prayer. The content of the recitation will, of course, be somewhat different for a person in the position of second language learner.

Narratives are generally one paragraph in length, but are not intended for memorization. The paragraph should provoke classroom language practice in the form of questions, answers and conversations ABOUT the paragraph. Narratives usually contain factual information about the culture that is of interest to the learner. Narratives can be taken from books, pamphlets and other primary sources, but they are frequently specially prepared with the language learner in mind.

Prose Passages are of no particular length, although they are frequently longer than either recitations or narratives. Prose passages are usually authentic language materials in that they are taken word-for-word from a primary source and they are not edited with the language learner in mind. For example, Prose passages can be unedited excerpts from a literary work. Vocabulary expansion and classroom discussion are primary objectives for a prose passage.

Operation

PURPOSE:

To introduce vocabulary and practice grammatical constructions (especially verb phrases) in the context of a natural or logical sequence of actions. The action sequence is frequently repeated on a regular basis in daily life so that each time the student performs the sequence of actions, the words that describe that sequence are available to him/her for sub-vocalization, or if appropriate, saying aloud.

BRIEF DESCRIPTION:

The students perform and talk about a series of actions that are associated with a process such as operating a piece of equipment.

SAMPLE OPERATION:

To use a cassette player/recorder:

First, push the eject button.

Then put the cassette in.

To record, push the play and record buttons simultaneously.

Push the stop button.

Push the rewind button.

To listen, push the play button.

PROCEDURE:

1. <u>Demonstrate</u> the operation to the students. Go through the entire operation once without stopping and have the students observe and listen.

2. Go through the operation again slowly. This time, <u>explain</u> <u>new</u> <u>words</u>.

3. Go through the operation again while <u>one</u> <u>of</u> <u>the</u> <u>students</u> <u>responds</u> to the commands with the proper action.

4. Teach the students the commands. Have them <u>repeat</u> the sentences several times for practice.

5. Have one of the students <u>give</u> <u>the</u> <u>commands</u> while a second <u>responds</u> with the action. If possible, divide the class into pairs and have each of them practice with a piece of equipment.

VARIATIONS:

1. Make a question for each step. After the student has completed the action, ask the question.

   For example:

   > Teacher: Push the eject button.
   > Student: (Pushes the button).
   >
   > Teacher: What did you do?
   > Student: I pushed the button.

   Note that you will have to teach the students the answer to each question. But you may not need to teach the question and that will allow you to go easily to the next step, which is:

2. Have one student give the command and ask the question while another responds and answers.

3. Have a third student answer the question.

   For example:

   > 1st Student: Push the eject button.
   > 2nd Student: (Pushes the button).
   >
   > 1st Student: What did he/she do?
   > 3rd Student: He/she pushed the button.

4. To help the students keep track of the sequence of actions, put a key word (usually the verb) from each step on the board.

5. After practicing the operation orally, have the students write it out.

6. Operations can be very effective review and summary
   exercises, especially for practicing verb phrases. You
   could do the following sequence for each step in the
   operation.

HABITUAL: What do you do first?
                First I Push the button.

COMMANDS: Push the button.
                (Pushes the button.)

PRESENT: What are you doing?
                I'm pushing the button.

PERFECT: What have you (just) done?
                I have pushed the button.

PAST: What did you do?
                I pushed the button.

FUTURE: What are you going to do next?
                I'm going to put the cassette in.

SUGGESTIONS AND GUIDELINES for Writing an Operation:

1. A good length is 6-10 steps (sentences).

2. Keep the sentence as short as possible.

3. Operations provide a good opportunity for practicing sequence words such as 'first,' 'next,' 'finally,' 'then,' etc. They also afford a good opportunity for practicing ordinal numbers.

4. Try to choose operations that the students will frequently encounter in daily life and encourage them to sub-vocalize the operation whenever they do it.

5. Some possible operations are:

    * Loading a camera
    * Taking a picture
    * Operating a language lab
    * Driving a car
    * Making coffee, tea
    * Cooking something with a recipe
    * Planting a garden
    * Making a long-distance phone call
    * Borrowing a book from the library
    * Filling out an application form

NOTE:

For more ideas see: Gayle L. Nelson and Thomas Winters, ESL Operations. Rowley, Mass.: Newbury House, 1980.

Mini-drama

PURPOSE:

To expose the students to colloquial language in the form of a drama script. The students are not expected to memorize or perform the drama, but rather use the script as a basis for building listening comprehension skills and exploring new forms of the language as it is used colloquially by native speakers.

BRIEF DESCRIPTION:

A mini-drama tells a little story and frequently involves several people, as opposed to a dialogue which is short, usually between two people and characterized by a lot of questions and answers. The drama can be excerpted from a literary work or purposefully written for the language class.

SAMPLE MINI-DRAMA:(Not a full length sample. See NOTE.)

Scholar 1: I have heard that some Europeans have again entered Bida. Could this be true?

Scholar 2: I have heard it is. They say the bature came along the river--along the Tsadda.

Scholar 3: They have now covered everywhere like Yajuju and Majuju. An Arab I met in Zango said that Egypt is now under their control.

Scholar 4: Not Egypt alone, even all of Hind.

Scholar 5: Yesterday a pilgrim from Mali was saying that a great Wangara warrior called Samure is resisting the French.

Scholar 6: May Allah make him successful.

All: Amin!

Scholar 7: Even now the Sultan of Istanbul is forced to consider these Europeans, otherwise...

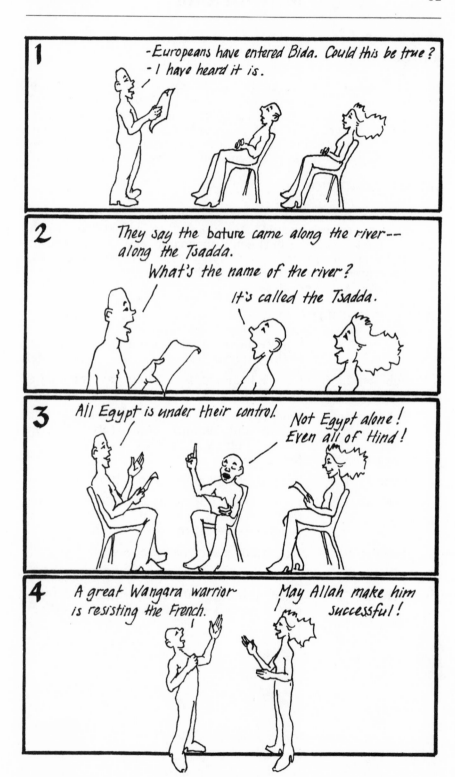

PROCEDURE:

1. <u>Read</u> the script to the students while they listen. At this point they should not see the written text so that they try to follow the conversation aurally. As you read, it may be useful to use pictures representing the characters and point to the character who is speaking as you read his lines.

2. <u>Ask</u> <u>and</u> <u>answer</u> questions about the script.

3. <u>Read</u> the script with the students. You can take one part and assign the other parts to the students. Encourage the students to read it dramatically.

4. Have the students <u>act</u> it out. A good procedure is to have them first <u>read</u> the line silently; then immediately look up and try to recite the line.

VARIATIONS:

1. If a tape recording of the drama is available, play the tape as the first step.

2. Another way to use a tape recording is to save it until you have done all the steps described on the previous page. Then play the tape and compare it with your classroom version.

3. Have the students practice the mini-drama several times and then present it to another class.

4. Have the students record their reading of the mini-drama and then play it back.

5. Select a topic and have the class write out a mini-drama.

6. Have the students re-state the plot in narrative form. They can do either an oral narrative or a written summary.

SUGGESTIONS AND GUIDELINES for Writing a Mini-Drama:

1. A good length for a mini-drama would be 25-50 lines.

2. If you choose to write your own mini-drama, a good source would be the interesting or humorous experiences a language learner might have in your culture.

3. Anecdotes such as those found in The Reader's Digest can serve as the basis for mini-drama plots.

4. If you choose a mini-drama from a real play, you may want to present it in segments over several days. By doing this, you may be able to do a complete one-act play.

NOTE:

The sample is excerpted from Shaihu Umar, a play by Umaru Ladan and Dexter Lyndersay adapted from the novel by Sir Abubakar Tafawa Balewa. (African Creative Writing Series) Longman: London, 1975.

Prose Passage

PURPOSE:

To use a passage of several paragraphs in length as the basis for 1) encountering new language forms 2) practicing the language by talking about the passage and 3) (incidentally) learning about the culture.

DESCRIPTION:

This technique is basically the same as the age-old practice of teaching the language through the use of readings. However, the recommended procedure as described on page 37, goes beyond reading comprehension, translation and vocabulary building, the usual practices associated with a prose passage. The emphasis is on building oral-aural skills by using a written passage as a conversation stimulus.

SAMPLE PROSE PASSAGE:

Dalarma is Sweden's folklore province. Here the bright folk costumes are still worn on festive occasions. Long Viking-style boats race across the lake to church on Sundays and the may-pole is joyfully raised in every farm and village at midsummer.

PROCEDURE:

1. Read aloud the entire passage once while the students follow along in the book.

2. As you read (slowly) the students should mark words and phrases they don't understand.

3. Have 3 (or 4) students read back to you only the words they have marked.

4. Listen and mark each word or phrase in your text. After the students have given their lists, you will be able to see which words and phrases are probably new to everybody. For example see the sample format for a piece of text that has been marked by the teacher.

5. Define the new words to the class.

6. Have the students define the remaining words to each other by asking each other questions in small groups.

VARIATIONS:

1. Have one or more of the students read the passage aloud.

2. Have the students read the passage silently, marking words and phrases they don't understand. Then have a show of hands to find out which words and phrases gave the most trouble.

3. After you have worked on the passage intensively, have the students summarize the passage in their own words.

4. Have the students translate the passage.

5. Have a discussion on the subject matter in the passage. If the passage is about some aspect of your culture, a useful discussion can be held on the comparative culture theme.

6. Have the students search for and bring to the class passages that are of interest to them.

SUGGESTIONS AND GUIDELINES for Writing a Prose Passage:

1. A passage of about one full page or less (double-spaced) would be a good length.

2. Although you can write the passage yourself, it is probably a better practice to find 'real' passages to work with.

3. A good source for these passages would be short entries in an encyclopedia.

4. If you are typing your own passage, double-space it to allow room for marking and writing between the lines.

Spiel

PURPOSE:

To bring into the classroom a short, spontaneous monologue that will serve as the basis for language practice, especially listening comprehension. A secondary purpose is to introduce the students to new vocabulary and grammatical constructions, and a final purpose is to give the students practice in learning how to learn from an exposure to raw linguistic data in the form of a native speaker's monologue.

BRIEF DESCRIPTION:

This technique is similar to a Narrative (see page 19) except that it is not written material; it is spoken and it is created in the classroom. Therefore, it resembles real speech more than a narrative does because it is produced spontaneously. There are several ways that a spiel can be used in the classroom, but the basic procedure is for the students to be able to comprehend and after practice, reproduce their own version of the spiel.

SAMPLE INSTRUCTIONS FOR A SPIEL:

Use as many of these words as you can in a 30-second talk about your family.

mother	grandfather	cousin
father	grandmother	living/alive
sister	uncle	dead
brother	aunt	married
		single

PROCEDURE:

1. <u>Plan</u> your spiel by studying the word list very briefly before you begin. Do not write it out.

2. <u>Give</u> the spiel. Have one of the students act as the timekeeper. He/she will stop you after 30 seconds. It is very important to stop, even though you may not say everything you wanted to. Talk at normal speed. Don't make it into a speech; keep it informal.

3. <u>Repeat the spiel</u>. It is all right to change it slightly, but do not make it longer or add new material. It is no longer necessary to be timed so you can slow down your speech somewhat as long as you don't add new material.

4. Allow the <u>students</u> to <u>ask questions</u> about the material. It may be useful to put some of the new words on the blackboard.

5. <u>Say the spiel</u> a final time at normal speed.

6. <u>Ask</u> the students <u>questions</u> about the material.

7. Ask one or more of <u>the students</u> to <u>give the spiel</u> as accurately as they can. If the spiel is difficult it is better to make this a group effort with everybody contributing what they know.

VARIATIONS:

1. A spiel can be done without a word list. The directions would give only the topic. For example, the directions might say: 'Talk for 30 seconds about town meetings in New England.'

2. A spiel could be based on a picture, with or without an accompanying word list.

3. To help the students recall the sequence of sentences in the spiel, put a key word from each sentence on the board.

4. As a final step you can have the students write out the spiel.

5. Have a student give a spiel.

6. Bring in a friend to give a spiel on some topic that he/she is familiar with.

7. Use a tape recorder to record the spiel. One advantage to a tape recording is that it will not change, no matter how many times you play it back.

8. You can also tape a brief news report from the radio and use it as the basis for the spiel.

SUGGESTIONS AND GUIDELINES for Developing a Spiel:

1. Ask the students to suggest spiel topics to you.

2. Spiels can be quite useful for building new vocabulary, but try to limit the new words. Adjust the length of the sentences to the level of the class. At the same time, try to keep the spiel as natural as possible.

3. Although the 30 second rule is somewhat flexible, it will usually produce a spiel of about 75 words, a reasonable piece of language for a class to work on.

4. Choose topics that are not too abstract. Some suggestions are:

   * My family
   * An occupation, trade or profession
   * A national holiday
   * A game or sport
   * A geographical area or region of the country
   * A daily routine
   * An art form such as folk music
   * A movie or play synopsis

NOTE:

This technique was developed by Earl W. Stevick.

Interview

PURPOSE:

To give the students the opportunity to listen to short
pieces of authentic language in a controlled fashion.

BRIEF DESCRIPTION:

The students act as interviewer and one or more
native speakers act as interviewees. The students
should have a prepared list of questions. The interviewee should respond naturally to the questions,
affording the students the opportunity to try to comprehend limited natural speech.

SAMPLE INTERVIEW FORMAT:

What is your favorite kind of music?

Why do you like _____?

Can you name some of your favorite pieces of _____?

Where can I hear _____?

Who is your favorite performer of _____?

Can you play a musical instrument?

Can you sing a _____ song?

PROCEDURE:

1. <u>Go</u> <u>over</u> <u>the</u> <u>prepared</u> list <u>of</u> <u>questions</u> with the students to be sure they understand them.

2. Have the students <u>practice</u> <u>saying</u> <u>the</u> <u>questions</u>.

3. Have the students <u>practice</u> <u>the</u> <u>questions</u> while you play the role of interviewee. Try this two or three times, varying your responses. Encourage the students to interrupt, ask for clarifications, repetitions, spellings, definitions, etc.

4. Invite one or more guest interviewees to class and <u>have</u> <u>one</u> <u>student</u> <u>act</u> <u>as</u> <u>interviewer</u>.

5. During the interview the other students should <u>take</u> <u>notes</u>.

6. After the interview <u>hold</u> <u>a</u> <u>question-answer</u> <u>session</u> where the other class members can ask questions.

7. Have the class <u>summarize</u> the interviewees' responses.

VARIATIONS:

1. Have the students prepare their own list of questions.

2. Have the students interview each other for practice.

3. The class can go on an interview field trip rather than bring interviewees to the classroom.

4. Appoint a class recorder who is responsible for collecting new words and phrases that emerge during the conduct of the interview.

5. Act as the interviewer and interview each of your students.

SUGGESTIONS AND GUIDELINES for an Interview:

1. Pick a specific subject and limit your questions to fact-finding questions.

2. Try to use all of the major question words with each subject (what, when, where, how, why, who).

3. Match your questions to subject matter areas that the students have some familiarity with.

4. Keep the interviews brief: 6-10 questions.

5. Some possible topics are:

   * Brief biographical information
   * Simple biographies
   * Daily routine
   * Occupations
   * Recreational/vacation preferences
   * Hobbies
   * Talents and skills
   * Sports
   * Ethnic background
   * How to make, cook, operate, perform something
   * Trips and travelling (My trip to Paris)

NOTE:

This technique is a modification of an idea suggested to me by Annie Hawkinson and adapted by Phil Sedlak.

Characters in Search of an Author

PURPOSE:

To practice using the language by talking about representative people from the culture. This technique may also be extended to a role-play format whereby the 'authors' (students) take on the personality of the character, and through the characters engage in dramatic interplay.

BRIEF DESCRIPTION:

Each student is given a picture of a person. The teacher initiates the lesson by giving some information about the person. Each student then provides similar information about his/her character. The students can then ask and answer questions and talk about each other's characters. This technique can be repeated over several days; each time it is done, new information is added and the characters gradually acquire a biography.

SAMPLE CHARACTER FORMAT:

This is John Everyman. He is 27 years old. He lives in Erewhon. He is an English teacher.

(The categories could be written on the back of the picture. Each class member writes in the facts for each category. Then each class member would make a short statement such as the model above.)

PROCEDURE:

1. Give every student (and yourself) a picture of a character.

2. Hold up your own picture and describe it with a few sentences.

3. Ask and answer questions after every sentence.

4. Tell the students to make up similar information about their own characters. It may be best to have the students write down the information (perhaps on the back of the picture). Then you can check the accuracy and cultural appropriateness of your students' sentences. For example, a student might say that an 18-year old woman lives alone, when in fact, this would never happen in your culture. These mistakes can be used as an opportunity to discuss your culture.

5. Each student in turn describes his/her character.

6. Ask the students questions about the characters. For example:

       1st Student: He is 18 years old.
       Teacher: How old is he?
       2nd Student: He is 18 years old.

7. Ask each student to describe somebody else's character.

VARIATIONS:

1. At the beginning of the lesson write your model sentences on the board for the students to refer to when they create their own sentences.

2. Have the student speak for the character. They would then practice 'I' and 'you' as well as 'he/she.'

3. As a final step, switch all the pictures and ask the students to describe their new character. If they cannot remember the correct information they must then ask the originator for it.

4. Set up a role-play situation (see Role-Play, p. 55) and have the characters interact with each other.

5. Pose a problem to the class and ask each student to express his/her character's opinion about the problem. Local and international current events would be a good source for these problems.

6. Periodically have the students write out in narrative form the biographies that are being developed.

7. This technique should be carried out over several days so that biographies can develop. Try it for 20 minutes a day for at least two weeks. By asking the students to assume the identity of their own characters, you may notice that this has a liberating effect on your students. They may be more willing to make mistakes, express opinions, and interact in a dramatic fashion.

SUGGESTIONS AND GUIDELINES for Developing Characters:

1. Magazines are a good source for pictures. Cut them out and paste them on stiff paper or cardboard.

2. Choose a variety of people, although it may be best to have characters that the students can readily identify with.

3. Listed below are some of the categories that you could use in describing the characters. In general, 3-5 items should be sufficient for any one lesson.

* name	* occupation
* age	* salary
* birthday	* educational level
* place of birth	* religion
* nationality	* hobbies
* language	* sports
* ethnic group	* interests
* family	* friends
* residence	* political beliefs
	* personality traits
	* hopes and dreams

Constructalog

PURPOSE:

To involve students directly in the language class by giving them the opportunity to write their own dialogues. By trying to write their material, the students will also encounter linguistic problems that might stimulate questions and investigations into the language.

BRIEF DESCRIPTION:

The students are given pieces of language (words, phrases and sentences) and asked to create a dialogue by using these pieces. Usually this is done with the students working individually, or in pairs or in small groups.

SAMPLE CONSTRUCTALOG FORMAT:

Use the words and phrases below to construct a dialogue between a sick student and a teacher. You do not need to use every word.

hurt	fever
pain	take a pill
ache	take temperature
stomach	give an injection/shot
headache	make an appointment

PROCEDURE:

1. Go over the list of words and phrases with the students to be sure they understand them and have some idea of how to use them. Have each student say a sentence using each word or phrase.

2. After the students understand the key words and phrases have them work individually or in small groups to write the dialogue.

3. Check each dialogue as it is being written. Point out errors and help the students, but don't be too obtrusive. The students should be allowed to make errors as they work; they can learn a lot from their mistakes.

4. Have the students practice their dialogues in pairs or small groups.

5. Have each group present its dialogue to the rest of the class.

VARIATIONS:

1. Don't provide a word list; let the students develop their dialogues from scratch. However, in order to keep the class as a whole focused on one semantic area, it may be best to give the class a topic, situation or problem to start with.

2. After each group has prepared and presented a dialogue, have the groups exchange dialogues and practice a new one.

3. Choose one of the dialogues and write it on the board. Have everyone learn it.

4. Have each group dictate its dialogue to the rest of the class so that everyone gets a copy of everyone else's work.

SUGGESTIONS AND GUIDELINES for a Constructalog:

1. About 12 words would be sufficient to guide the students in writing their own dialogues.

2. Have the students limit their dialogue to 12 lines or less.

3. Choose topics, situations and problems that will be relevant to the students.

4. Some possible dialogue situations are:

* at a bank	* at a gas station
* at a post office	* at a bus station
* at a theatre box office	* in a police station
* at a doctor's office	* in a bar
* in a store	* in a taxi
* in a restaurant	* at customs/ immigration

NOTES:

1. The basic idea of this technique, having the students write their own material, can be extended to other formats besides a dialogue.

2. This technique should not be attempted until the students have some familiarity with the language. They should use the target language not their native language as they work together preparing the material.

Role-play

PURPOSE:

To put the students into a realistic communication situation to 1) sharpen their listening comprehension skills, 2) bring them in contact with new language, and 3) discover areas where they need additional practice.

BRIEF DESCRIPTION:

There is no pre-established language sample for this technique, only a set of instructions that initiates a conversation. Usually the conversation/role-play is between the teacher and one or more students.

SAMPLE ROLE-PLAY FORMAT:

You have just moved into your new apartment and your neighbor knocks on your door to introduce him/herself.

PROCEDURE:

1. Explain the situation.

2. Select the "cast." Usually it is best to cast yourself in one of the key roles.

3. If a tape recorder is available, have one of the students record the role-play.

4. Have the other students take notes. A simple system is to have the student note-taker construct a log of the conversation, noting only the opening words of each new line and if possible, the last word of each line (See Notes).

5. Role-play the situation. Try to let it develop naturally. Don't let it go on too long: 1 or 2 minutes is sufficient.

6. Re-play the tape. Pause after each utterance for questions and answers. If the students don't have any questions, ask simple questions such as "What did he say?"

7. Gradually re-construct a written version of the role-play, using the tape and/or the log.

VARIATIONS:

1. Have two students do the role-play while you listen for errors. Do not interrupt the role-play while it is in progress. During the re-play, comment on and correct the students' sentences.

2. After doing the role play once, select a new cast and do it again. Have one of the students take your role.

3. Add a new element to the instructions, one that will force the role-play to take a slightly different direction.

4. Discuss any cross-cultural communication problems that may have arisen during the role-play.

5. Combine this technique with Characters in Search of an Author (see p. 47).

6. Use the written re-construction of the role-play as a Mini-Drama (see p. 31).

SUGGESTIONS AND GUIDELINES for Developing a Role-Play:

1. Be careful that the role-play doesn't go on too long. Too much material can over-load the student with too many new words, phrases and constructions. Learners can only deal with a limited number of new pieces of information at one sitting.

2. Some possible role-play situations are:

   * a social visit in a home
   * interviewing a job applicant
   * asking to borrow something
   * turning down an invitation gracefully
   * a visit to a doctor or dentist
   * firing an employee
   * reporting a stolen or lost item
   * helping an accident victim or sick person
   * accepting a ride as a hitch-hiker
   * returning a defective item to a store

NOTE:

   To facilitate the keeping of a role-play log, use a form like the one below to help keep track of the flow of the conversation.

Line #	VISITOR (teacher)	HOST (Raoul)	
1	Excuse me ... neighbor.		
2		Hello ... come in.	
3	My name ... Brown.		
4		My name ... Smith.	
5	Nice to meet ..		

Valuations

PURPOSE:

    To stimulate conversation practice using subject matter which is of high interest to the student.

BRIEF DESCRIPTION:

    The students are asked to state their likes (or dislikes) in the form of a simple list. Then they compare and talk about their lists.

SAMPLE VALUATIONS FORMAT:

    A: List your five favorite TV programs, starting with your first choice.

        1. _____

        2. _____

        3. _____

        4. _____

        5. _____

    B: Use the grid to list your and your classmates' five favorite TV programs.

	1	2	3	4	5
Teacher					
Jon					
Kathy					
Susannah					

PROCEDURE:

1. <u>Present</u> <u>the</u> <u>question</u> to the students. A simple kind
   of valuation activity is to ask the students to:

   List your 5 favorite _____s.

2. Allow the students time to think about and <u>construct</u>
   <u>their</u> <u>lists</u>.

3. Have each person (you should usually include your-
   self) simply <u>read</u> <u>his/her</u> <u>list</u> while the others listen.

4. Have the students <u>ask</u> <u>and</u> <u>answer</u> <u>questions</u> <u>and</u>
   <u>discuss</u> each other's lists.

5. <u>Listen</u> for words and phrases that the students need
   or can't handle properly. Note them down, slip them
   into the discussion wherever possible, and call the
   students' attention to them when the discussion is
   over.

VARIATIONS:

1. Have the students suggest topics for valuation.

2. Have the students put their lists on the blackboard for
   quick reference.

3. After each student reads his/her list, have another
   re-state it. This will focus attention on the need to
   listen carefully.

4. Keep a few notes as the lists are being read and then
   quiz everyone briefly with questions such as:

   Who likes _____?

   Does John like _____?

   Does anybody like _____?

   How many people like _____?

5. Have each student construct a grid (See Sample
   Format) to record everyone's list.

6. At the end of the discussion have each student write a
   short summary of the discussion.

SUGGESTIONS AND GUIDELINES for Developing Valuations:

1. If the activity goes slowly, try reducing the list to 3 items. This may be especially necessary with larger classes. Keep in mind that the activity can be overwhelmed by too much information.

2. Some possible lists are:

   * food/drinks/restaurants
   * books/magazines/authors
   * movies/movie stars
   * cities/states/countries
   * TV programs/TV stars
   * hobbies/interests
   * sports/sports teams
   * academic subjects
   * pieces of music
   * automobiles
   * politicians

3. It is probably best to start with items that are not too controversial.

NOTE:

The valuation list described as the basis for this technique is only one very simple activity. A useful reference for other activities is: Sidney B. Simon, Leland W. Howe and Howard Kirschenbaum, Values Clarification. (New York: Hart, 1972).

Substitution Drill

PURPOSE:

To help the students get a feeling for a particular sentence pattern or grammatical construction by forcing the repetition of the basic sentence while at the same time producing semantic variations of the sentence by changing some part of it.

BRIEF DESCRIPTION:

The teacher says the basic sentence (frame) and adds a word that is to be substituted (cue) in the proper place in the sentence. There are several varieties of Substitution Drills. In some kinds the substitution item forces a change elsewhere in the sentence (subject-verb agreement, singular-plural agreement, gender agreement). In another major variety, sometimes called the multiple slot substitution drill, there is more than one kind of word being substituted.

SAMPLE SUBSTITUTION DRILL:

A. Single-slot.

I have a <u>book</u>.

1.	pencil	5.	notebook
2.	pen	6.	piece of chalk
3.	ruler	7.	piece of paper
4.	eraser	8.	envelope

B. Multiple-slot.

The <u>rain</u> in <u>Spain</u> <u>stays</u> mainly on the plain.

1.	falls	5.	sleet
2.	snow	6.	France
3.	Italy	7.	is
4.	Switzerland	8.	fog

VARIATIONS:

1. The teacher, after giving the model, gives only the single word substitution.

    Teacher says: Students respond:
      Pencil.   I have a pencil.
      Pen.   I have a pen.

2. Vary the drill from choral responses (everyone responds at once) to individual responses.

    Teacher says: The class responds:
      I have a book. Pencil.   I have a pencil.

      I have a pencil. Pen.   One student responds:
                                       I have a pen.

3. Have the class echo the response in unison.

    Teacher: Student: The class:
      I have a book.
      Pencil.   I have a pencil. I have a pencil.

4. Have one of the students conduct the drill.

    Student: Other student(s):
      I have a book. Pencil.   I have a pencil.

5. Use actual objects or flash cards with pictures of the single word.

    Teacher: Student(s):
      I have a book.
      (Holds up pencil or   I have a pencil.
      picture of pencil)

6. Write single words on the blackboard and point to them for substitutions.

    Teacher: Student:
      I have a book.
      (Points to word pencil)   I have a pencil.

NOTE:

Substitution drills are fairly easy to do as choral exercises.

SUGGESTIONS AND GUIDELINES for Writing Substitution
        Drills:

1. The basic sentence should not be long. 8-10 words is a good length.

2. About 20 items is a good number.

3. You can write circular drills so that by the time you come to the last item the sentence has returned to the basic frame you started with. This allows you to keep right on going with the drill if you want to go through it a second or third time.

4. In writing multiple slot drills be very careful that the slots are quite distinct from each other. In other words, two noun slots, such as a subject noun and an object noun, would lead to confusion.

5. Some grammatical points that can be practiced through the use of these drills are:

   * subject-verb agreement (a substitution drill can be a conjugation drill put in the context of a complete sentence).

   * word order--by repeating the same sentence pattern several times, the word order can be fixed in the student's mind.

   * increasing the students' awareness of parts of speech--by forcing the students to pay attention to features such as noun slots, verb slots, adjective slots, etc. the students can pick up a greater awareness of the parts of speech of the substitution items.

   * gender or noun class agreement--by substituting a noun of a different gender or noun class in a sentence, other words and concords may have to change to agree with the new word.

   * singular-plural distinctions--alternating singular and plural nouns in the noun slot may force changes in agreement elsewhere in the sentence.

Expansion Drill

PURPOSE:

To give the students the opportunity to make more complex sentences. This technique is especially useful for helping the students learn how to add modifying words, phrases and clauses.

BRIEF DESCRIPTION:

The teacher provides a set of instructions that tell the students to add a new element to a basic sentence and make all the necessary changes that the new element will cause. The teacher then gives the basic sentence and a student gives the response. An optional step (shown as part of the procedure) is to have the entire class echo the correct answer, thus giving everyone the opportunity to say every sentence.

SAMPLE EXPANSION DRILL:

Add the word "always" to these sentences.

Mrs. Jackson is busy. > Mrs. Jackson is always busy.

1. John is here
2. He drinks coffee.
3. Steve and Tim are late.
4. Fire engines are red.
5. The weather here is beautiful.
6. She smokes a pipe.
7. We drive to work.
8. Susan types well.
9. Shirley is in the library.
10. I am tired.
11. He reads Newsweek.
12. They work on Saturday.
13. London is foggy.
14. It rains in Calcutta.
15. She answers the phone.
16. They watch television.

VARIATIONS:

1. Change the kinds of student responses, alternating between choral responses where everyone answers at the same time to individual responses.

2. To correct a mistake, don't give the correct version to the student. Simply signal that the response is incorrect and allow the student the opportunity to correct it.

3. Two or three different items can be used for expanding the sentence. The teacher can put the items on the blackboard and point to the element to be added to the sentence. Flash cards and oral cues can also be used.

   The teacher puts on the board:

   never   always   usually   frequently

   The teacher says:

   John is here. (points to never)

   The student responds:

   John is never here.

4. The opposite of an expansion drill is a <u>REDUCTION DRILL</u>. The procedure for doing a reduction drill would be basically the same as the expansion drill. A reduction drill would require the students to reduce one part of a sentence to a shorter form. Typically, this would involve teaching pronouns, contractions and other words that represent longer expressions. Samples:

   They do not like rock music. >
                              They don't like rock music.

   John and Maria are gone. > They are gone.

   See page 72 for suggestions and guidelines.

NOTES:

1. Simple expansion drills (like the sample) work well with choral responses, but more complicated expansions are better done with individual responses.

2. In the given sample, there is very little semantic connection from one basic sentence to the next. This is because the point of the drill is to focus the learner's attention on a grammatical feature rather than involve the learner in a communicative exchange of information.

SUGGESTIONS AND GUIDELINES for Expansion Drills:

1. 12-20 sentences is a good length.

2. Choose vocabulary which is familiar to the students. Stopping to explain new words interferes with the point of the drill--working on grammar.

3. Notice in the sample format that the student is forced to choose where to insert the new element. In sentences 1, 2, 4, 5, 9, 10 and 13, the new element is inserted after the verb, while in the other sentences the new element is inserted before the verb. The point here is that the drill is constructed so that the student has to stay on his toes and consider each response carefully. In other words, mindless repetition or substitution will not be a successful tactic in this drill. In writing drills, vary the sentences to force active participation by the students.

4. An occasional humorous or unusual sentence can add life to the drill, but don't over-do it. Remember again that the point of the exercise is to focus attention on a grammatical feature.

5. Although the sentences in expansion (and reduction) drills in most textbooks are not connected to each other in meaning, if you are writing your own drills, it would be a good idea to have some kind of thematic unity to the sentences. For example, all the sentences could deal with a general theme such as "shopping" or "travelling."

6. Expansion drills can be used to:

   * add a frequency word (always, never, often, etc.)

   * add adjectives (big, small, long, etc.)

   * add prepositional phrases (at the bank, in this room, etc.)

   * add time phrases (in the morning, today, etc.)

   * add a relative construction (Do you know that...)

SUGGESTIONS AND GUIDELINES for Reduction Drills:

1. Some points that can be practiced are:

   a. noun   >   pronoun
       (John >   he)

   b. Full form   >   contracted form
       (I do not have   >   I don't have)

   c. locative phrases   >   locative adverbs
       (in this room   >   here)

2. In practicing contracted forms, it may be best to concentrate on having the students understand rather than speak the contraction, especially when practicing colloquial forms such as "gonna" for "going to." If so, it may be better to present the contracted (reduced) form and have the students respond with the full form.

Chart Pattern Practice

PURPOSE:

To practice a sentence pattern through repetitions of the pattern. The sentences are constructed by the students from visual cues.

BRIEF DESCRIPTION:

A chart containing a series of pictures is used as the basis for practicing a particular sentence pattern or grammatical structure. Usually the pictures are set up in a series so that the students can proceed from one picture to the next without cues from the teacher.

SAMPLE CHART:

LOOK AT THE CHART.

Yesterday Jim got up at seven o'clock.

VARIATIONS:

1. Use a question and answer chain, rather than just one
   sentence.

   T: What time did Jim get up yesterday?
   S1:   He got up at 7 o'clock.
   T: What time did he take a shower?
   S2:   He took a shower at 7:15.
            etc.

2. After completing the chart, ask questions about the
   pictures in random order.

3. The same chart can be used to practice several types
   of patterns. Each time a new pattern is practiced,
   previous patterns can be reviewed.

4. Have each student recite all the sentences.

5. Have the students give a personal variation on the
   original to practice "I/you" patterns. In other words,
   a student might say: "Yesterday I got up at 8:00."

NOTE:

   When a chart is used for the first time, it may be
   necessary to go through it once to introduce the new
   vocabulary.

SUGGESTIONS AND GUIDELINES for Writing Chart Pattern
Practices:

1. It's easy to make your own stick-figure charts. A
   good chart needs only 6-10 frames. Some themes for
   the charts are:

   * daily routine

   * weekend routine

   * school-day routine

   * specific job routines

   * a trip to someplace

   * going to a movie

   * performing some specific task

   * an operation (see p. 25)

2. Some patterns that can be practiced are:

   Everyday/yesterday/tomorrow Jim...(tenses)

   While Jim was...(coordinate actions)

   Jim...but I...(negatives)

   Before Jim...he...(sequential actions)

3. The charts do not have to have a time sequence. They
   can also be related thematically. For example, a chart
   of athletic activities showing baseball, basketball,
   football, soccer, etc. could be used to practice sentences expressing preference, ability, comparison, etc.

   Other themes are:

   * various arts

   * types of transportation

   * recreation activities

   * occupations

   * academic subjects

Utterance-Response Drill

PURPOSE:

To have the students repeat a sentence pattern or a special expression several times. By changing the words, the repetition is less tiresome. Idioms and formulaic speech can also be practiced in the context of this drill.

BRIEF DESCRIPTION:

This drill is like a two-line dialogue where the teacher makes the utterance and the student responds. The student is expected to respond with a particular sentence pattern.

SAMPLE UTTERANCE-RESPONSE DRILL:

Respond to the questions with the following pattern:

Sure, I'd love to. _____ is great fun.

For example:

How would you like to play tennis?

Sure, I'd love to. Playing tennis is great fun.

1. How would you like to dance the cha-cha-cha?
2. How would you like to go to the movies?
3. How would you like to sing folk songs?
4. How would you like to drink beer with me?
5. How would you like to take a walk?
6. How would you like to go fishing?
7. How would you like to read poetry?
8. How would you like to listen to folk songs?
9. How would you like to play the guitar for us?
10. How would you like to look at my slides?
11. How would you like to visit Uncle Paul?
12. How would you like to study grammar?

VARIATIONS:

1. The students can make the utterance, as well as the response.

2. You can have two possible responses, and the student can choose one.

   Sure I'd love to. _____ is great fun.

                      OR

   Yeech! _____ is boring.

3. You can have a 3-part utterance, with the third student taking the opposite response.

   T: How would you like to ski?

   S1: Sure, I'd love to. Skiing is great fun.

   S2: Yeech! Skiing is boring.

4. Provide a list of expressions and let the student choose one.

   Sure, I'd love to.

   Right on!

   Yes, of course.

   Great idea!

   Now you're talking!

   Why not?

SUGGESTIONS AND GUIDELINES for Writing an Utterance-Response Drill:

1. These drills can teach both a grammatical feature and idiomatic expressions. The idiomatic expressions could be omitted, but the drill would become much less interesting. In fact, this kind of drill may be more effective for teaching idioms than it is for teaching grammar.

2. Write two-line exchanges that will also be useful for teaching intonation. Have the students say the sentences dramatically. For example:

   A: John finally passed chemistry.

   B: At last! I didn't think he'd ever pass!

3. Not all utterances and responses are question-answer. Some can be statement-statement and some can be statement-question. For example:

   Statement: John will never pass chemistry.

   Statement: Not a chance! He's terrible at chemistry.

   Statement: John will never pass chemistry.

   Question: Why in the world is he so bad at chemistry?

NOTE:

   For more information and English examples see: Jason B. Alter, Roy W. Collier and Miho Tanaka Steinberg, Utterance-Response Drills. Englewood Cliffs, N.J.: Prentice Hall, 1966.

Transformation Drill

To give the students practice in producing major sentence types. Attention is focused on the structural relationships between sentences types, and the changes (transformations) that are necessary to convert one type of sentence to another.

BRIEF DESCRIPTION:

The students are given a sentence with instructions to change the sentence in a particular way.

SAMPLE TRANSFORMATION DRILL:

Make the following sentences negative:

1. I like pears.
2. He wants a camera.
3. They understand Spanish.
4. You need a haircut.
5. I have a dictionary.
6. She owns a camera.
7. They know all the answers.
8. He has a lot of money.
9. Susie speaks Spanish.
10. We need a dictionary.
11. They have my camera.
12. She wants to go.
13. I know the answer.
14. He likes to study Spanish.
15. They want more money.
16. You have my dictionary.

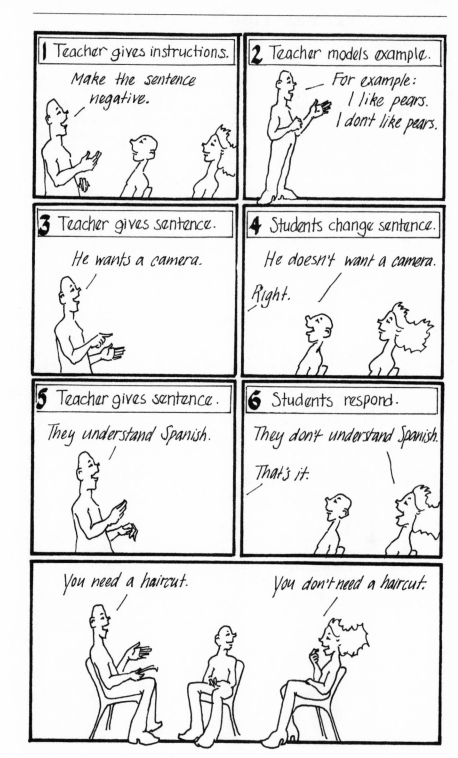

VARIATIONS:

1. After an individual gives an answer, you can ask the whole class to "echo" the student's answer in unison.

2. After the first student changes the sentence into its new form, have the second student change it back to the original.

> T: He wants a camera.
>
> S1:   He doesn't want a camera.
>
> S2:   He wants a camera.

3. Students can conduct the drill. One student reads the basic sentence and a second one changes it.

NOTES:

1. See the Grid Drill (p. 85) for a more complex transformation drill.

2. The vocabulary in the sample is purposefully limited to common words so that it doesn't get in the way of practicing the transformations. One way to limit the vocabulary is to use the same words several times, as in the sample.

SUGGESTIONS AND GUIDELINES for Transformation Drills:

1. Some typical kinds of transformations are:

   Statement   >   Question

   Affirmative   >   Negative

   Affirmative question   >   Negative question

   Active   >   Passive

   One tense   >   Another tense

   Singular subject   >   Plural subject

   Formal commands   >   Informal commands

2. About 15-20 sentences should be sufficient for the practice. When dealing with a particular transformation for the first time, keep the sentences short and simple.

3. Because the focus is on grammar, restrict the vocabulary of the sentences to words the students should know.

Grid Drill

To review various sentence types and verb tenses. The grid can be used as a cumulative review exercise, repeating the exercise and expanding on it as a new form is introduced.

BRIEF DESCRIPTION:

The students look at their grid while the teacher gives them a cue. They respond with a sentence that fits the teacher's cue. There are four possible cue types (refer to grid below).

Verb:	go, see, like, etc.
Person:	John, we, they, etc.
Type:	affirmative, negative, question, etc.
Tense:	today, yesterday, tomorrow, etc.

SAMPLE GRID:

	AFFIRMATIVE +	NEGATIVE −	QUESTION ?	
Everyday				
Today				
Yesterday				
Tomorrow				

85

VARIATIONS:

1. The cues and instructions can be varied in a number of ways. Try several combinations.

2. Make a large grid for the wall and point to the cues rather than speaking them.

3. Try the exercise occasionally as a rapid-fire game/quiz.

4. Have the students write the responses to the cue.

5. A student can lead the class.

NOTES:

1. It is a good idea to develop a series of symbols such as these:

    +   =   affirmative

    -    =   negative sentence

    ?   =   question

    wh   =   question-word sentence

    ,?   =   tag question

2. The tense expressions can also be developed into one word or short phrases such as:

    yesterday   =   past tense

    have just   =   present perfect tense

    tomorrow at 2 o'clock   =   future continuous

3. Warning: there will probably be places where the grid will not work. For example, imperative forms do not fit easily into the grid. Obviously the grid should not be used for forms that will cause confusion.

4. The students do have the opportunity to put in some sentence elements of their own. In the sample, one student responded with "there" and the second student chose to respond with "Boston."

SUGGESTIONS AND GUIDELINES for Writing a Grid Drill:

Although the grid will have to be adapted to fit the language, the sample below for English should provide some ideas.

	+	−	?	−?	+,−?	−,+?
everyday (simple present)						
now (present progressive)						
yesterday (past)						
going to (future)						
will (future)						
have just (present perfect)						
all week (pres. perf. progr.)						
yesterday at 2:00 (past progr.)						
going to/yesterday (going to-past)						
used to (past habitual)						
should, etc. (modal simple)						
should have, etc. (modal past)						

Key
+   affirmative statement
−   negative statement
?   question
−? negative question
+,? negative tag question
−,? affirmative tag question

Translation

PURPOSE:

The process of translating from one language to another will increase the student's awareness of the grammar of the target language, and for that matter, his own language as well. Translation can also be used to diagnose a student's weaknesses or test his proficiency or achievement.

BRIEF DESCRIPTION:

Translation can be done in two directions: from the target language to the native language or the reverse. The first type requires the student to comprehend a target language sentence. The second type requires the student to produce a target language sentence. In the sample format below, the native language is assumed to be English and the target language French. Therefore, this is a comprehension exercise (from target to native).

SAMPLE TRANSLATION EXERCISE:

Traduisez les phrases suivantes:

1. Je vais acheter un livre.
2. Elle va visiter Hawaii.
3. Ils ne vont pas venir demain.
4. Nous allons jouer au basket.
5. Est-ce que vous allez dîner?
6. Il ne va pas voir le film.
7. Nous allons regarder la télévision.
8. Est-ce que tu vas venir?
9. Je ne vais pas parler au directeur.
10. Elle va visiter la ville.
11. Vous n'allez pas dîner au restaurant.
12. Tu vas prendre un café.
13. Ils vont se reposer.
14. Je vais me baigner.
15. Est-ce que nous allons partir à 6 heures?

(Comprehension Exercise)

(Production Exercise)

VARIATIONS:

1. Having done the drill in one direction, it can be repeated in the other direction. In general it is best to do the comprehension type first and then follow with a production exercise.

2. Each sentence can be done in both directions. For example:

> T: Je vais acheter un livre.
>
> S1: I'm going to buy a book.
>
> T: (OPTIONAL STEP) I'm going to buy a book.
>
> S2: Je vais acheter un livre.

3. The students can be asked to write the response rather than speak it. This procedure is better for diagnostic or testing purposes than it is for practice.

4. The format can also be in the form of a paragraph, rather than a list of sentences. In this format, however, it would be best to do only comprehension exercises.

NOTES:

1. The instructions can still be given in the target language, as in the illustration.

2. This technique can only be used in a bi-lingual setting. It cannot be used where the students represent several linguistic backgrounds.

SUGGESTIONS AND GUIDELINES for Writing Translations:

1. If the translation is for the purpose of practicing a particular grammatical structure, the sentences should, of course, all contain that structure and they should contain a minimum of other potential problems. In other words, decide what you want to practice and then write sentences that will focus on the point of the practice. Note in the sample format that the "going to" future is the point of the practice and the remainder of the sentence (the frame around "going to") is quite simple.

2. If the point of the translation is to diagnose student weaknesses, then the sentences should contain a wide variety of grammatical structures.

3. If the translation is used to assess a student's proficiency, then the sentences should contain a range of grammatical structures from simple and easy to complex and difficult.

4. For the purposes of achievement testing, the sentences should contain only those grammatical structures which have been previously studied.

Question-Answer Practice

To have students practice affirmative and negative sentences in response to a question. This requires the student to comprehend the question and make the necessary transformation of the question to a statement.

BRIEF DESCRIPTION:

The teacher informs the students of what kind of answer is expected (long, short; affirmative or negative) and then poses questions for the students to answer.

SAMPLE QUESTION-ANSWER PRACTICE:

Answer the following questions with "Yes" and a long answer.

For example: Do you like avocados? >

Yes I like avocados.

1.   Do you know Martha?
2.   Does she like ice cream?
3.   Does she dance well?
4.   Do they speak Spanish?
5.   Do I talk slowly?
6.   Do we work hard?
7.   Does John own a radio?
8.   Do you drink beer?
9.   Do we know them?
10.   Do I read the newspaper?
11.   Does Martha know John?
12.   Does it rain here often?
13.   Do they smoke cigarettes?
14.   Do you have a dollar?

VARIATIONS:

1. The practice can be repeated with different kinds of answers, such as:

    Answer with a short answer

    Answer with both a short and long answer

    Choose an answer (yes or no)

2. Mix the answers by giving the student either a yes or no cue. For example:

    Teacher: Do you know Martha? Yes.

    S1:   Yes, I know Martha.

    Teacher: Do you want an ice cream. No

    S2:   No, I don't want an ice cream.

3. After doing the practice successfully, have the students construct their own questions, and conduct the practice in a chain pattern of:

    S1: Question A.

    S2: Answer A; question B.

    S3: Answer B; question C. etc.

NOTE:

There may be occasional pronoun confusion with question-answer practices. For example the answer to a "we" question could be "we" or "you."

SUGGESTIONS AND GUIDELINES for Writing a Question-Answer Practice:

1. It is best not to mix different question types in one practice. Some question types would be:

    Yes-No questions

    Tag questions

    Wh- questions (what, when, who, etc.)

    Either-or questions

2. To make the practice more interesting write questions which pertain to the class and its individual members (as in the sample).

3. It is a good idea to establish a theme for each practice and have all the questions pertain to that theme. This will reduce the likelihood that unexpected vocabulary will confuse the students.

Visual Question-Answer Practice

PURPOSE:

> To use visual information (pictures) as a basis for practicing questions and answers and/or specific grammatical constructions. A secondary purpose can be to learn some new vocabulary.

BRIEF DESCRIPTION:

> An illustration containing several related items (see Sample Format) is the basis for this practice. The teacher introduces a question-answer exchange and then has the students carry on with the exchange.

SAMPLE FORMAT:

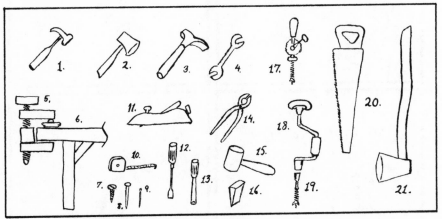

1.	hammer	8.	nail	15.	maul
2.	hatchet	9.	brad	16.	wedge
3.	adz	10.	tape measure	17.	drill
4.	wrench	11.	plane	18.	brace
5.	clamp	12.	screw driver	19.	bit
6.	bench	13.	chisel	20.	saw
7.	screw	14.	pliers	21.	ax

> Q: What is number _____?
> A: It's a/an _____.
>
> Q: What is a/an _____ used for?
> A: It's used for _____.

VARIATIONS:

1. Once the basic pattern has been established, have the students ask the questions as well as give the answers.

2. This practice can be done as a "chain" practice. For example:

      1st Student: Asks questions.
      2nd Student: Answers.

      2nd Student: Asks questions.
      3rd Student: Answers.

      3rd Student: Asks questions.
      4th Student: Answers.

        etc.

3. Use the picture without the key list of words and have the students write down the key words as they are introduced.

4. After practicing the patterns for a while, cover up the key word list and have the students try to remember the key words.

NOTES:

1. This practice is very similar to a Cummings Device (see p. 11). The difference is that this practice makes no attempt to be conversational or simulate conversational exchanges. The patterns to be practiced are selected for their grammatical construction rather than their communicative potential.

2. This practice can also be very useful for teaching technical or specialized vocabulary.

SUGGESTIONS AND GUIDELINES for Writing Visual Question-Answer Practices:

1. A good format is two questions with their corresponding answers, although faster classes can probably handle at least one more question-answer pair.

2. Twenty items is a comfortable number of items to work with.

3. If you can't draw your own sketches, look for composite illustrations in an encyclopedia.

4. Another excellent source for illustrations is the Duden pictorial dictionaries. For an example, see The English Duden (Mannheim: Bibliographisches Institut).

5. A wide variety of grammatical constructions can be practiced through the use of this technique. Some possible questions that could be asked about the sample illustration are:

   Do you have/own a _____?

   Have you ever used a _____?

   Why would you use a _____?

   Which tool is better for _____?

   How much do you think a _____ costs?

   If I want to _____ what should I use?

Question-Word Analysis

PURPOSE:

To give the students practice in comprehending a sentence. Secondarily, the students will increase their awareness of the parts of a sentence and will increase their ability to respond to and use the basic question words (what, who, when, where, why, how).

BRIEF DESCRIPTION:

The teacher reads a sentence and then asks question-word questions about it. The students respond with short answers. Each short answer is also part of the sentence. All the short answers together form the entire sentence. This practice takes the sentence apart and (optionally) puts it back together again.

SAMPLE FORMAT:

Listen to the sentence and answer the questions with short answers.

1. John is walking to the library.

    a.   Who is walking to the library?
    b.   What is he doing?
    c.   Where is he walking to?

2. He usually studies in the library for two hours.

    a.   Who studies in the library?
    b.   Where does he study?
    c.   How long does he study?
    d.   How often does he study in the library?

3. John doesn't go to the library on Saturdays.

    a.   When doesn't he go to the library?
    b.   Where doesn't he go on Saturdays?
    c.   Who doesn't go to the library on Saturdays?

4. Yesterday he wrote a term paper on art for Professor Smith.

    a.   What kind of paper did he write?
    b.   What was the paper on?
    c.   Who did he write it for?
    d.   What did he do?
    e.   When did he do it?

VARIATIONS:

1. After the questioning, ask a student to recite the entire sentence.

2. Read the sentence and have one of the students pose the questions to a second student, who answers and then questions the third student in chain-fashion.

3. Emphasize one part as you read the sentence and have the students form the question for the emphasized part. For example:

   T: John is <u>walking</u> to the library.

   S: What is John doing?

4. "Yes/No" and "either/or" questions can also be used.

NOTES:

1. This technique can be useful for teaching long sentences which are difficult to reproduce from memory after having heard them only once.

2. The sentences can form part of a longer passage, and the passage can be taught as a Narrative (see p. 19).

3. It is not a good idea for the students to respond to the questions with full sentences (except as the final step). Fragments are better because they indicate that the student has in fact understood the question.

SUGGESTIONS AND GUIDELINES for Writing a Question-Word Analysis:

1. Virtually any sentence in the language can be subjected to a question-word analysis. Therefore, model sentences are everywhere, although descriptive sentences are probably the best type. Sentences from a dialogue are somewhat more difficult to use than sentences from a prose passage.

2. Some key question words and phrases are:

Things	What
	Which
People	Who
	Whom
Purpose	Why
Time	When
Place	Where
Manner	How
Frequency	How Often
Size	How Large
Distance	How Far
Qualities	What Color
Quantity	How Many

Action Chain

PURPOSE:

To practice grammatical structures in the context of simple actions associated with sentences.

BRIEF DESCRIPTION:

The students and teacher carry out a series of actions and talk about the actions. The series of sentences that accompany the action follow the sequence of command, question and answer.

SAMPLE ACTION CHAIN:

_____, look at _____.

What are you doing?
I'm looking at _____.

Say _(hello)_ to _____.
__(Hello)__ .

What did you do?
I said hello to _____.

VARIATIONS:

1. Ask a third student "he/she" questions.

>   T: S1, look at S2.   S3, what is S1 doing?
>   S3:   He's looking at S2.

2. Have a student give the commands and ask the questions.

3. Have two people perform the chain and ask "you (plural)/we" questions.

4. Have two people perform the actions and ask "they" questions.

5. Have the students work together in pairs or small groups.

NOTES:

1. This technique is useful for practicing several pronoun forms and several verb tenses all in one sequence.

2. These actions must be done deliberately so that the students' verbal and physical responses are co- ordinated.   It can be confusing to say "What are you doing" when the action has been completed and the correct response would be in the past tense.

3. This is a good technique for both introducing and practicing action verbs.

SUGGESTIONS AND GUIDELINES for Writing an Action Chain:

1. Some classroom activities could be:

    giving and taking something
    writing and erasing on the board
    standing and sitting
    walking, running, jumping
    speaking, mumbling, singing, humming
    opening and closing doors and windows
    turning on and off the lights

2. A sequence for practicing the future tense is:

    T: S1, please _____. Wait!
          What are you going to do?

    S1: I'm going to _____.

3. A possible long sequence could be:

    command: Stand up!
    past tense question: What did you do?
    past tense answer: I stood up.
    command: Sit down! Wait!
    future tense question: What are you going to do?
    future tense answer: I'm going to sit down.
    present tense question: What are you doing right now?
    present tense answer: I'm sitting down.
    present perfect question: What have you just done?
    present perfect answer: I have just stood up and sat dow

Spontaneous Pattern Practice

PURPOSE:

To practice a sentence pattern that uses information created by the student. The personal involvement on the students' part makes the practice much more interesting and memorable.

BRIEF DESCRIPTION:

The teacher gives a model sentence that contains some blanks. The teacher inserts personal information in the blank and then through a series of questions, has each student create a sentence of his own. The students' own sentences then become the basis for further questions and answers.

SAMPLE FORMAT:

If I had a thousand dollars, I would _____.

VARIATIONS:

1. The teacher asks each student about the other students' sentences.

2. Have the students ask "you" questions (S5, What would you do?)

3. Have each student ask "he/she" questions (S5, What would S2 do?)

4. Have each student ask "who" questions (who would go to California?)

5. Have each student tell what all the other students would do.

6. Have the students write all the sentences they have created.

NOTES:

1. The students may make mistakes as they create a sentence. The teacher should correct the sentences. One way to correct is to ask a question, emphasizing the incorrect part. For example:

   S: I would go to the California.

   T: You would go to the California?

2. Keep the practice limited to one sentence per student.

3. Have the students keep a notebook of these practices. It will help personalize their language course.

SUGGESTIONS AND GUIDELINES for Writing a Spontaneous Pattern Practice:

This practice is good for working on verb phrases, especially complicated phrases.

Some samples are:

Yesterday I _____.

Tomorrow I'm going to _____.

Last year at this time I was _____.

If I had _____, I would _____.

Yesterday I was going to _____, but _____.

_____ isn't in class; he might be _____.

Last night I was _____ when _____.

Instead of _____, I wish I could _____.

Whenever I _____, I _____.

Yesterday I wanted to _____, but I couldn't because I had to _____.

I really ought to _____, but I would rather _____.

Manipulations

PURPOSE:

To give the students the opportunity to practice a limited amount of the language (and hence a limited number of grammatical structures) in a meaningful conversational way.

BRIEF DESCRIPTION:

The focus is on objects which can be brought into the classroom. The teacher sets up a situation which requires the students to manipulate the objects and talk about the objects and the manipulations.

SAMPLE FORMAT:

Use the following objects: a book, a pen, a pencil, a notebook.

Questions: Who has a _____?
              Who doesn't have a _____?

Answers: I
              You
              He   don't   has   a   ____.
              She   doesn't   have
              We
              They

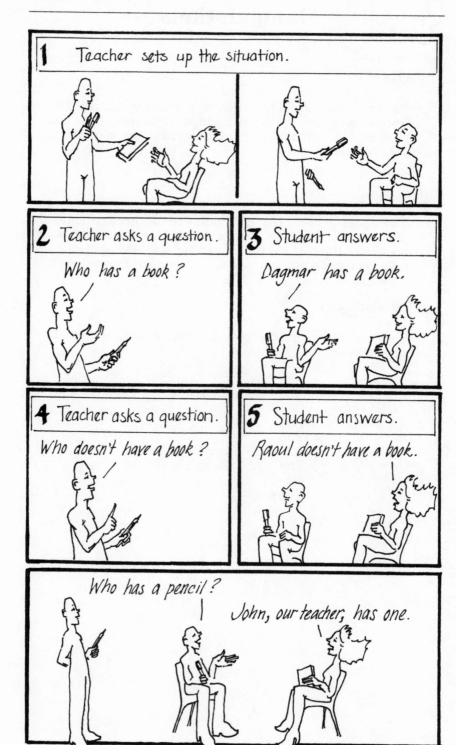

VARIATIONS:

1. After introducing the basic pattern, let the students carry on with all the questions and answers. As the teacher, you step aside from the role of class leader to listen and correct.

2. Tell the students before you begin that once the basic pattern has been introduced, you will not interrupt with corrections. It will be up to the students to ask for confirmations and corrections if they need it.

3. Have the students seated in a circle facing outward so that they cannot see each other. Give everyone an object and have them find out what everyone has by asking and answering questions. If there are 8 students, allow a maximum of 7 questions about each object.

NOTE:

The Silent Way approach to language teaching uses a bag of multi-colored wooden rods of varying sizes, similar to those used for teaching math to children. These rods have advantages in that they are highly portable, inexpensive and abstract enough to be used in a wide variety of situations.

SUGGESTIONS AND GUIDELINES for Writing Manipulations:

1. Collect a box of "things" for props. It is easy to build a large collection of small things such as pencils, tacks, matches, paper clips, rubber bands, stamps, envelopes, etc. You could make thematic collections (office things, natural things such as sticks, stones, seeds, household things, classroom things, etc.)

2. The objects can be useful for teaching the grammar of the noun phrase. For example:

    a. Gender or noun classes.

    b. Agreement of nouns and adjectives.

    c. Singular and plural forms.

    d. Count and non-count nouns.

    e. Word order of modifying adjectives.

    f. Definite and indefinite articles.

3. Some basic sentences that can be used are:

    a. Questions and answers such as:

        Do you have, need, want, like, see, etc.

        Who has, wants, needs, etc.

        What does _____ want, need, like, etc.

    b. Commands and responses such as:

        Give _____ to _____.

        Take _____ from _____.

        Lend _____ to _____.

    c. Descriptions such as:

        I have a large green grammar book.

Transition Techniques

Transitions in the classroom occur at three points: At the beginning of a teaching session, in the middle when there is a change from one activity to another, and at the end, as the teaching session comes to a close. Transitions can be disruptive, but they can also be productive. The following transition techniques can be used to minimize disruption and turn potentially unproductive time into useful classroom activities.

OPENERS

TECHNIQUE: **Scrambled Sentences**

PURPOSE: To start the class with an activity that minimizes the interruptions of late-comers.

PROCEDURE: Cut 3x5 index cards into quarters. Write a sentence, putting each word in thesentence on a spearate quarter. Write a number in the upper right corner or on the back — the same number for each word in the sentence, for example:

$Have^3$	you^3	$ever^3$	$seen^3$	the^3	Taj^3

$Mahal^3$	$?^3$

Scramble the sentence and put a rubber band around the cards. Put 6-8 different sentences in a pile on a table. The students, as they enter the classroom, working alone, or in pairs, take a sentence to their seats, unscramble it, and write it down on a piece of paper. When the first student has unscrambled all the sentences or all the students have arrived in class, stop the activity and go over the answers.

TECHNIQUE: **Scrambled Sentences**

PURPOSE: Students often sit in the same seat, day after day, sitting next to someone they feel comfortable with. There is nothing wrong with this, but from time to time they should sit beside and work with someone they don't know.

117

PROCEDURE: Write out a sentence that contains one word for each member of the class. Put each word on a separate slip of paper, e.g.

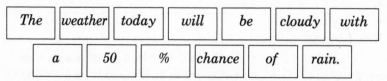

| The | weather | today | will | be | cloudy | with |
| a | 50 | % | chance | of | rain. |

Scramble the slips of paper. As the students come into the classroom, give them each a slip of paper with one of the words. They have to consult with each other to unscramble the sentence and seat themselves in order, according to the word order of the sentence. When everyone is seated, they call out their words, one after another to form the original sentence.

TECHNIQUE: **The 50-Word Essay**

PURPOSE: To begin the class on time with an activity that is useful for the early-comers and requires the late-comers to also do the work— as homework, if necessary.

PROCEDURE: Write a topic on the board. As each student comes into the classroom, he/she is supposed to immediately start writing whatever he/she can about the topic, producing a minimum of 50 words. As the late-comers arrive, they start to work. When the students who have arrived on time finish, check their work and stop the activity. Late-comers and others who have not finished have to complete the writing for homework and submit it the next day before they can enter the class.

Keep the topics light and lively, for example: Skiing, penguins, a great movie, hamburgers, smoking, the Rolling Stones.

CHANGERS

TECHNIQUE: **Bean Bag Trivia Quiz**

PURPOSE: To change the pace of the class by introducing a mildly competitive, slightly physical activity.

PROCEDURE: Write a topic, e.g. countries, on the board. Then pose a question about the topic, e.g. "What's the largest country in the world in land area?" Toss the bean bag to a student who tries to answer the question. The student then asks another question based on the topic and throws the bean bag to someone else. If the first student answered the question correctly, he/she is eligible to receive another "toss." If he/she couldn't answer the question, he/she still asks one question, but is ineligible for future "tosses." The competition continues until a winner (or winners) is declared.

TECHNIQUE: **Line-Up**

PURPOSE: To use a non-competitive physical activity to change the pace.

PROCEDURE: Prepare three or four "line-up" commands which will force the students to line up in the classroom from front to back in a particular order. Give the command and then allow the students a few minutes to mill around and arrange themselves in order in a line. Some examples of commands are: Line up tallest to shortest; lightest to heaviest; smallest hometown to biggest hometown; biggest family to smallest family, etc. When the line-up is complete, each student makes a statement about his/her position, e.g., "I am 6 feet, 2 inches, and I'm the tallest in the class."

TECHNIQUE: **Would You Please**

PURPOSE: To change the pace with a fast-action command-response game (a variation of "Simon Says").

PROCEDURE: Tell the students you will give them a series of commands. They obey and perform only those commands that are preceded by the phrase "Would you please." Then start everyone off with "Would you please stand up." When everyone is standing, continue the commands rapidly, occasionally dropping "Would you" or "please" or the whole phrase. Students who obey incomplete commands, sit down. Continue until one person remains standing. Good verbs for the commands are: Touch, look at, point to, pick up, put down, turn, open, close.

CLOSERS

TECHNIQUE: **Perfect Recitation**

PURPOSE: To end a class with a short exercise that permits the students who perform perfectly to take a break or leave for the day.

PROCEDURE: Establish a short text (3-5 sentences) that the students need to recite perfectly. If the student makes an error, stop him/her immediately and go to another student. When a student gives a perfect recitation, he/she may leave the classroom. Recitations can be short descriptions of a picture, short dialogues or short spiels with "yesterday," "today" and "tommorrow," e.g., "Yesterday Carlos went to a movie. Today he is attending class. Tommorrow he's going to go to the city." Recitations can also be brief summaries of the preceding class session.

TECHNIQUE: **Unbroken Circle**

PURPOSE: To end the class in a perfect performance in which every person in the class must do something perfectly to earn the class the right to leave or take a break.

PROCEDURE: Establish an order, for example, from left to right around the room, if the class is in a semi-circle. Give an utterance to student #1, who must respond with a grammatically perfect response. If the response is correct, student #2 makes a response, etc. When an error is made, the circle is broken and student #1 has to begin the responses again. The responses continue until all have responded perfectly, without breaking the circle. Some sample utterances: Where were you born? When did you arrive in ____? How did you get to ____? What were you doing this morning at 8 a.m.? What will you be doing tomorrow at 10 p.m.? If I gave you a hundred dollars, what would you buy?

TECHNIQUE: **Card Collecting**

PURPOSE: To end the class period with a short game that requires student-student interaction.

PROCEDURE: Choose a category, for example famous scientists, and write the first name on one card and the last name on another card, e.g. Albert Einstein . Make enough cards so that each student will have at least four cards. Shuffle the cards and give each student four. Then the students move around the room, comparing cards. When a match is made, the two students bring their matched cards to you for verification. Take the cards if the match is correct. The game is continued until all the cards are matched. Students can leave when they have matched all four of their cards. Do not allow general questions such as "Who's got Albert?" They can only talk directly to each other. Other categories could be: country-city; synonyms; antonyms; two-word verbs; verb + particle; idioms, etc.